THE LIBRARY OF
AMERICAN
LIVES AND TIMES

PETER STUYVESANT

New Amsterdam and the Origins of New York

L.J. Krizner
Lisa Sita
THE NEW-YORK HISTORICAL SOCIETY

The Rosen Publishing Group's
PowerPlus Books™
New York

Published in 2001 by The Rosen Publishing Group, Inc.
29 East 21st Street, New York, NY 10010

First Edition

Book Design: Laura Murawski

Library of Congress Cataloging-in-Publication Data

Krizner, L. J.
    Peter Stuyvesant : New Amsterdam and the origins of New York / L. J. Krizner and Lisa Sita.— 1st ed.
      p. cm.— (The library of American lives and times)
    Includes bibliographical references (p.) and index.
    ISBN 0-8239-5732-2 (lib. bdg.)
    1. Stuyvesant, Peter, 1592–1672—Juvenile literature. 2. Govenors—New York (State)—Biography—Juvenile literature. 3. New York (State)—History—Colonial Period, ca. 1600–1775—Juvenile literature. 4. New Amsterdam—Biography—Juvenile literature. [1. Stuyvesant, Peter, 1592–1672. 2. Govenors. 3. York (State)—History—Colonial Period, ca. 1600–1775.] I. Sita, Lisa, 1962– II. Title. III. Series.
    F122.1.S78 K75 2001
    974.7'02'092—dc21   00-010930

Manufactured in the United States of America

CONTENTS

1. Who Was Peter Stuyvesant?

The origins of New York, one of the busiest and most cosmopolitan cities in the United States today, reach back over 350 years. Before New York was called New York, it was the Dutch town of New Amsterdam, founded in 1624. Although New Amsterdam lasted only forty years, the Dutch presence in America was to influence culture in the Northeast for centuries to come. An important part of the Dutch legacy handed down to the present day is the story of New Amsterdam's most well known leader, Petrus, or Peter, Stuyvesant.

New Amsterdam, located at the tip of Manhattan Island, started as a company town. As part of the larger Dutch colony of New Netherland, New Amsterdam was established and controlled by the Dutch West India Company. This was an enterprise formed to pay for new settlements and to operate outposts for business and trade. In an attempt to make New Netherland a

Opposite: This oil painting of Peter Stuyvesant was painted by Henri Couturier between 1660-1663 on a wood panel. Stuyvesant was born sometime near the beginning of the seventeenth century. During his director-generalship of New Netherland, he became something of a legend due to his temper and the strict rules he imposed.

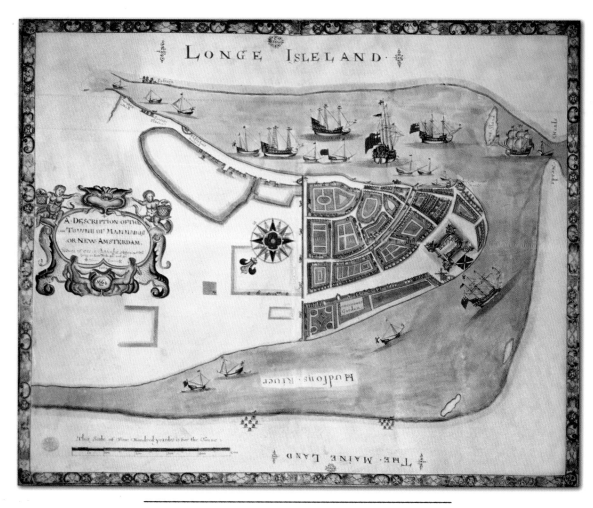

This plan of Manhattan, Long Island, the Hudson River, and New Amsterdam was created in 1664. New Amsterdam was formed as a central place for the Dutch to live and conduct trade. Living in a smaller community rather than spreading out into the surrounding countryside provided protection from Indians and made it easier to get news and supplies from the trade ships that frequented the harbor.

profitable trade settlement, the Dutch West India Company needed to find a leader who could monitor and control the colonists. Finally, the Dutch West India Company hired Peter Stuyvesant as director-general of the colony of New Netherland in 1647. He would become the fifth and final director-general of the colony, not the first, as many believe.

Today Stuyvesant is sometimes characterized as a strict, unforgiving leader. He is remembered as someone who ruled with an "iron fist" while stomping through the streets of New Amsterdam on his wooden leg. History books sometimes give him the unflattering nickname of Peg-Leg Pete, and historical paintings usually show his stern side, portraying him with frowns and furrowed brows, always angry. In 1809, the New York writer Washington Irving portrayed Stuyvesant as saying, "If

© Collection of the New-York Historical Society/1865.4

This marble bust of Washington Irving was made by Erastus dow Palmer in 1865. Irving lived from 1783-1859.

© Collection of the New-York Historical Society/23724

This engraving of Diedrich Knickerbocker by an unknown artist was dedicated to Washington Irving by the publishers of his *History of New York*.

Washington Irving was a famous author born in 1783. Some of his most well-known works include Rip Van Winkle *and* The Legend of Sleepy Hollow. *He also wrote the satirical, or comical,* A History of New York, *that helped make Stuyvesant a legend. To write this story Irving used the pen name Diedrich Knickerbocker. For a long time people believed Knickerbocker was a real person. The name Knickerbocker has become synonymous with any person who can trace their ancestry back to the original Dutch settlers, or even just someone who has lived in New York their whole life. It is also where the New York Knicks took their name.*

ever I catch thee, or any of thy tribe, meddling again with affairs of government, by Saint Nicholas! But I'll have every mother's b—— of ye flea'd alive, and your hides stretched for drumheads, that you may thenceforth make a noise to some purpose." Irving helped to create the image of an always-firm Stuyvesant that survives to this day.

Stuyvesant was indeed a self-willed and unbending leader. At the same time, he was also an energetic director-general who loved the colony. He hoped to improve living conditions and make the colony prosperous, as it once had been. Stuyvesant was more than just director-general of New Amsterdam. He was a competent employee of the Dutch West India Company, a war hero, a husband, and a father.

When Peter Stuyvesant first arrived in New Amsterdam in 1647, the colony was in terrible condition. A lack of strong leaders had allowed the business of the colony and the everyday lives of the colonists to deteriorate. The streets were filthy, buildings were in disrepair, and dishonest business was being conducted. People were hopeful that this new director would bring opportunity and growth, and so the colonists received Stuyvesant with joy. They were happy to have this famous war hero, who had lost his leg in battle on the Caribbean island of St. Martin, as leader of the colony.

Stuyvesant, in turn, began his new job with charismatic energy. In an effort to bring organization to

New Amsterdam, Stuyvesant made important changes that improved business and brought order to the colony. He immediately made rules for the colonists to follow, such as setting curfews and forbidding pubs to open on Sundays. His decisions and instructions were not always popular with the people. He became infamous for his dictatorial and often domineering ways, and the colonists began to resent him. He enforced only his own ideas about how things should be done. He didn't ask the people what they wanted. Instead he did what he felt was best.

Stuyvesant is known to have said, "I shall reign over you as a father governs his children." Indeed, Stuyvesant may have inherited his stern way of governing from his father, Balthazar. Balthazar Stuyvesant was a Dutch Reformed minister in the Netherlands, and he raised his son in the strict tradition of his religion. Peter's religious beliefs and strong moral code were so deeply ingrained that it was difficult for him to separate his personal convictions from his professional life. Therefore, Peter's way of leading the colony was heavily guided by his Dutch Reformed views. He truly believed he was acting in the best interests of the colonists.

Peter spent his schoolboy years in the town of Scherpenzeel in the Netherlands, and grew up around ships, ports, and the sea. He was surrounded by exciting news from distant lands, and he desired to sail

© Collection of the New-York Historical Society/1858.28

"Peter Stuyvesant and the Trumpeter (The Wrath of Peter Stuyvesant)" was painted by A.B. Durand in 1835. It is an oil on canvas. Asher B. Durand is best known for his landscapes, but earlier in his career he did a number of portraits and literary scenes. In this painting, Durand has captured a scene from Irving's *History of New York* in which Stuyvesant has just learned of the Swedish capture of Fort Casimir.

the seas from a very early age. In hopes of holding an important position when he was older, he was diligent with his studies. His hard work and adventurous spirit led him to a military career, after which he worked for the Dutch West India Company. The Company

This is the Dutch West India Company's house on the Rapenburg Canal. This building was the center of operations for the Company's holdings in the Caribbean and America. All decisions were made by a board of nineteen men who were in charge of overseeing employees like Stuyvesant. Luckily for Stuyvesant, news traveled slowly so he was able to issue his ordinances without interference.

recognized his willingness to work hard and sent him to serve in the Caribbean as a clerk and later as governor. Here he proved himself to be dedicated, courageous, and committed. So, with trouble brewing in New Amsterdam and the great need for a leader, the West India Company decided that their trustworthy and devoted employee, Peter Stuyvesant, was the perfect candidate for the job.

2. Masts on the Horizon

Peter Stuyvesant was sent to establish order in the Dutch colony of New Netherland in 1647, but why had the Dutch come to North America in the first place? The answer begins nearly two hundred years earlier in Europe.

The second half of the fifteenth century marked the beginning of an exciting and dangerous time in the history of Europe. Trade was flourishing and kings and queens paid explorers to find new trade routes on the then unknown and largely uncharted seas. Trade routes over land were already well established, and such exotic items as spices and silks from the East had found their way into European markets. In 1499, Vasco da Gama, a Portuguese explorer, reached India by sailing from Portugal along the western coast of Africa, around the Cape of Good Hope, and into the Indian Ocean, opening up a new sea trade route to Asia.

A few years before, Christopher Columbus's voyage to the New World in 1492 had sparked interest on the other side of the globe, opening up new possibilities for

This is a portrait of Vasco da Gama, a Portuguese navigator. Vasco da Gama was born in about 1469, in Sines, near Portugal. He was chosen by King Manuel I to find a new sea route to India. In 1498, after more than five months of sailing, he succeeded in his quest. However, due to the hostility of Muslim merchants, he was unable to establish a trading station there. He returned to Portugal in 1499.

This map by Juan de la Cosa shows Africa as it was known in 1500, after Vasco da Gama's expedition. The boats traveling around the coast of Africa show the general route that da Gama took on his way to India.

trade and exploitation of natural resources. Driven by the search for gold, Spain was the leading power controlling the New World. By the end of the sixteenth century, Spain and Portugal together had established a large and prosperous empire in the Americas, profiting mainly from the production of sugar and later the slave trade. Spain kept control of this new empire with its powerful fleet of ships, known as the Spanish Armada.

While Spain and Portugal were enjoying prosperity, countries in northern Europe, including France, England, and the Netherlands, were looking for ways to make their own profits in both the East and the West. The turning point came in 1588, when the Spanish Armada tried to invade England and was defeated by the British navy. With Spain no longer holding the monopoly on trade, other countries, including the Netherlands, now had a better opportunity for prospering in their own trading ventures with Asia. The Netherlands seized this opportunity and quickly became the leader in trade with the East. They were so successful, they formed the Dutch East India Company in 1602 to manage their business. As for the New World, the defeat of the Armada also ended Spain's control over the Atlantic Ocean and opened up the way for other countries to set out for the Americas.

The Netherlands and Spain were now in competition for trade. However, relations between the countries had been stormy long before this time. The Netherlands, a Protestant nation, had been rebelling against Catholic Spanish rule for over thirty years. In an age of religious intolerance, where Europe's ruling monarchs were divided between Catholics and Protestants, the Netherlands was renowned for its openness in matters of religion. It was a haven for people fleeing persecution in

This 1598 hand-colored woodcut shows the *Vanguard,* a British ship, attacking the Spanish Armada. The defeat of the Spanish Armada was a huge breakthrough for global trade. It also marked the rise of power for England that would continue for more than a century.

their homelands. Consequently, the Netherlands became a mosaic of peoples, including Calvinists, Jews, Huguenots, and Puritans. Many of these people were the ones who later colonized New Netherland.

In 1609, Spain called a twelve-year truce to the ongoing war with the rest of Europe, which, for the Netherlands, began a period of great achievement in business, art, and science. The Dutch excelled at shipbuilding and trade, which brought great wealth into the country. By the time Peter Stuyvesant came to New Amsterdam, the Netherlands had become the richest country in Europe, enjoying what is known as its Golden Age. Amsterdam was a center of art and education, as well as the busiest port on the continent. Prosperous merchants built fine homes, and employed artisans to make fine furniture from imported woods. Artists were commissioned to paint scenes of this luxurious new life. It was a period when great artists like Rembrandt and Vermeer were at the height of their careers, learned men experimented with the laws of nature, and schools and universities flourished.

As the Netherlands began its climb to power, the young Dutch East India Company started looking for a

© Collection of the New-York Historical Society/1951.414a-c

These stained glass windows were probably created by Evert Duyckinck around 1656. The windows were created for a building in Beverwyck, or present-day Albany, but eventually made their way to 8th Street in New York City. Windows like these were typical of the time and would have been found in many places in Amsterdam and New Netherland. Note the stained glass window in the painting on the opposite page.

"Young Woman with a Water Pitcher" was painted by Dutch painter Jan Vermeer sometime between1662-1665. Vermeer was one of the many artists who flourished during Amsterdam's Golden Age.

more profitable way to do business. The Company hoped to find a shorter route to the East, and for this they hired the English sea captain Henry Hudson. Hudson set sail from Amsterdam in 1609 on his ship the *Half Moon* in search of a northwest passage to Asia. The route he took to North America was influenced by

This picture shows Manhattan as it appeared before the arrival of the Dutch colonists. Native American villages like this one were probably encountered by Henry Hudson as he sailed up the North River (present-day Hudson River) looking for the Northwest Passage. Although he did not discover a path to the Pacific Ocean, he did discover that North America was rich in resources and would offer valuable trading opportunities for the Dutch.

other explorers who had sailed there before him. Giovanni Verrazano had sailed to the mouth of what is known today as the Hudson River, and Hudson's friend

John Smith had made a voyage to the English colony of Jamestown, Virginia.

When Hudson reached North America, he sailed along the coast, stopping for repairs and to trade with the Indians. He then brought the *Half Moon* up the river that now bears his name. The ship sailed as far as present-day Albany, where Hudson realized that the river did not lead to the Pacific Ocean. Although Hudson did not find a shorter route to Asia, reports of his voyage aroused the interest of Dutch merchants. According to these accounts, beaver pelts and other furs could be traded from the Indians at low prices. Independent merchants began sending ships to the area Hudson had explored, which soon became known as New Netherland. In 1614, the Dutch fur trader

Beaver pelts were stretched on a wooden frame like this as part of the tanning process used to soften animal hides into leather.

© Collection of the New-York Historical Society/1939.105

This model of Hudson's boat, the *Half Moon*, was created by an unknown maker between 1825-1900 out of wood, metal, canvas, paint, and string.

Before returning to Amsterdam after his voyage to America in 1609, Hudson first stopped in England. When the English government realized how profitable Hudson's findings were for the Dutch, they refused to let him return to Amsterdam or sail for any country except England. In August 1610, funded by the Muscovy Company of London, Hudson set out on another voyage to find the Northwest Passage. Ten months later his crew rebelled. The crew put Hudson, his son, and a few loyal sailors on a raft and set them out to sea. They were never heard from again.

This view of New Amsterdam, the capital of New Netherland, clearly shows the fort, windmill, and busy harbor.

Hendrick Christiansen built Fort Orange, just south of present-day Albany. In 1621, the Dutch West India Company was formed, creating a monopoly in trade in America, Australia, and the West Coast of Africa. The Company's employees were men and women who left the Netherlands to settle in these new Dutch colonies.

In 1624, the Dutch West India Company sent its first settlers to New Netherland. The group of thirty Walloon families, French-speaking refugees from southern Belgium, was made up of 110 men, women, and children. The Company sent with them livestock,

This hand-colored woodcut shows the landing of the Walloons in New Amsterdam in the 1600s.

seeds, and farm equipment to begin the new settlement. Most of the settlers were brought to Fort Orange, but some were left at Governor's Island, in what is now New York Harbor, and other areas along the river. More settlers arrived in 1626. New Netherland was now established as a fur-trading colony with New Amsterdam as its capital. The Dutch influence in America had begun.

3. Cultures in Contact

When the Dutch arrived in North America, there were many groups of Indian peoples living in the Northeast. Some spoke the Iroquoian languages and some the Algonquian languages. The people living in the area of New Amsterdam were the Delaware, known in their own Algonquian language as "Lenape." The Lenape were made up of many smaller groups, like the Esopus, Hackensack, Raritan, and Canarsee. Their homeland stretched along the Atlantic Coast and included areas that are now present-day New York, Pennsylvania, Delaware, and New Jersey.

The Lenape lived in villages made up of extended families. Houses in Lenape villages were built on frameworks of saplings covered with bark. Depending on the size of the family living inside, a house may have been a "longhouse" or a smaller, domed dwelling, called a "wigwam." The Lenape shared the responsibility of making decisions in their communities. Leaders were chosen, but they did not have power to tell people what to do. Rather, they were usually respected elders

This drawing of a Lenape couple was created by a Swedish settler in 1690, after the Lenape had been pushed out of lands occupied by the Dutch. The arrival of the Dutch settlers aggravated competition between the Lenape and other tribes, like the Mohawk and Iroquois. Between 1630 and 1635, the Susquehannock launched a brutal war against the Lenape that drove them all the way to southern New Jersey and Delaware. The Lenape lost half of their population and as a condition of peace became the subjects of another tribe.

who acted as counselors, offering advice and guidance on important matters.

Lenape women cared for homes and raised children. They grew corn, beans, squash, and other plant foods in their gardens. They also gathered wild plants to be used for food and medicines and raw materials for making such things as baskets and mats. They made clothing from the tanned hides of deer and other animals.

Men hunted the abundant wildlife of the forests, including white-tailed deer, rabbits, and bears. They fished in the rivers in dugout canoes made from whole trees, and harvested shellfish, like clams, mussels, and crabs, from the ocean. They made tools and weapons from stone, wood, bark, horn, and shell.

Belief in the supernatural played an important role in Lenape life. The Lenape believed that spirits, called *manetuwak*, were present in all things and often appeared to people in dreams and visions. The spirits were sacred to the Lenape, therefore all things in nature were also considered sacred, including land, sky, and water. Nature was considered a gift given by the Creator to be shared by all. Nature could not be owned by individuals. People, plants, and animals all had an equal

Photo courtesy of the Rochester Museum and Science Center, Rochester, New York

This photograph shows, from left to right, a bone needle, a brass needle, a bear canine, and a brass thimble. The Indians might have used bone and metal tools such as these for sewing or decoration. However, the brass tools would not have been introduced until after they began trade with the European settlers.

Photo courtesy of the Rochester Museum and Science Center, Rochester, New York

Flint points, perforated and triangular brass points, and iron and flint knife blades like these were typical hunting tools used by the Indians. Metal objects became valuable items in trade because they were much more durable than the Indians' customary tools made of stone and bone.

right to it. Families were free to use the land and waters to plant, hunt, fish, and gather other needed resources. After they had farmed the land for several years and used many of the resources in their area, the Lenape would leave their villages and build new ones elsewhere.

The Europeans arriving in America had different ideas about land. In Europe land was valuable personal property bought and sold between individuals. Whenever land was purchased, an official deed was drawn up stating who owned the property. When the Dutch first arrived in New Netherland, they needed land on which to settle, so they began to offer gifts to the native peoples in exchange for land. This seemed reasonable to the Lenape. Whenever the Lenape made agreements with one another or with other tribes about who would use a certain area of land, it was their custom to exchange gifts

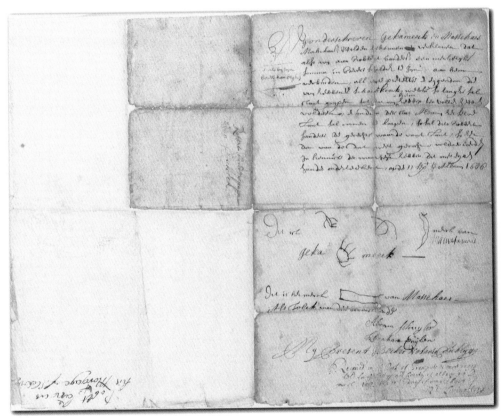

This deed for Indian lands in colonial New York, near Albany, was signed in 1686. This reflects a typical deed that would have been created and signed whenever the Dutch purchased land from the Native Americans. The Indians signed the deeds with symbols from their own language. The Lenape tribes spoke Algonquian with three different dialects: Munsee, Unami, and Unalactigo.

as a sign of good will. By accepting gifts from the Dutch, the Lenape were agreeing to let the Dutch use the land. They believed that eventually the Dutch would move to another area, just as they themselves did.

The Dutch had different ideas. Employees of the Dutch West India Company were required to draw up a deed, which they signed, whenever they bought land from the Indians. Sometimes the Indians also signed these deeds by marking them with symbols of their names. These documents were a European tradition, so the Indians probably did not fully understand the meaning of what they were signing. However, to the Dutch, the land they had received from the Lenape was legally theirs and they had no intention of giving it up.

The relationship between the Dutch and the Lenape began as a friendly one, based on trade. The

In the 1920s, a deed was discovered stating that the Dutch bought Manhattan Island from the Lenape, but this deed later proved to be a forgery, or fake. No real deed has ever been located.

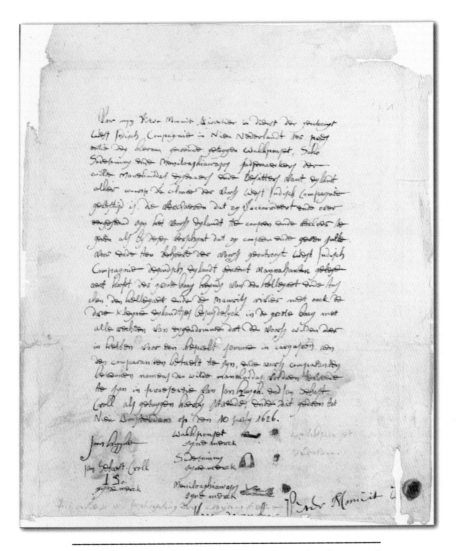

Historians believed this deed for Manhattan Island was a legitimate document for many years. It was eventually proven to be a fake.

Lenape received goods in return for the beaver furs they provided to colonists. In the Netherlands, these furs were used to trim garments and make muffs. Even more importantly, the fur was processed into a kind of felt needed for wide-brimmed hats fashionable

© Collection of the New-York Historical Society/71357

This engraving by an unknown artist shows Dutch trading with Indians at Manhattan. The Dutch settled in America to exploit the valuable resources found there. Trading with the Indians was easier than trying to compete directly with them in hunting and farming, especially in what must have seemed a hostile landscape to the Dutch. Sometimes trading was beneficial to both parties, but often the settlers took advantage of the Indians who were not familiar with European ideas of ownership.

at the time. However, whenever different cultures meet, misunderstandings almost always arise. For the Dutch and the Lenape, misunderstandings were sometimes over land rights.

Contact with Europeans brought other problems for the Lenape. The Lenape were not the only people who wanted to do business with the Dutch. Sometimes disagreements over who would control trade led to wars

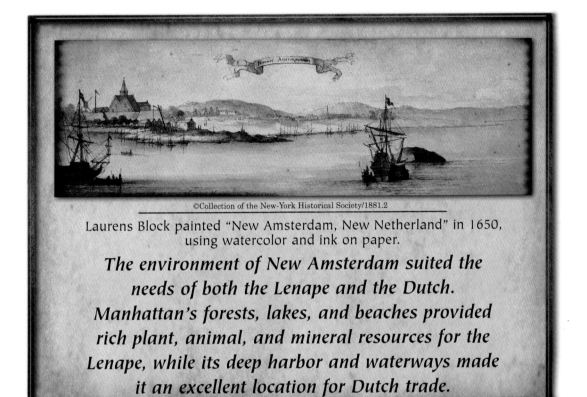

©Collection of the New-York Historical Society/1881.2

Laurens Block painted "New Amsterdam, New Netherland" in 1650, using watercolor and ink on paper.

The environment of New Amsterdam suited the needs of both the Lenape and the Dutch. Manhattan's forests, lakes, and beaches provided rich plant, animal, and mineral resources for the Lenape, while its deep harbor and waterways made it an excellent location for Dutch trade.

between native groups. Also, as trade increased so did European settlements, pushing the Lenape out. They started living in areas occupied by other tribes, and had to compete for food and other resources. After awhile they found themselves facing attacks from the more powerful Mahicans and Iroquois to the north. Contact with Europeans also brought new diseases to the Lenape. European diseases like smallpox and measles killed many, and the Lenape population dropped drastically. By the time Peter Stuyvesant came to New Netherland, relations between the Dutch and the Lenape were not as friendly as they once had been.

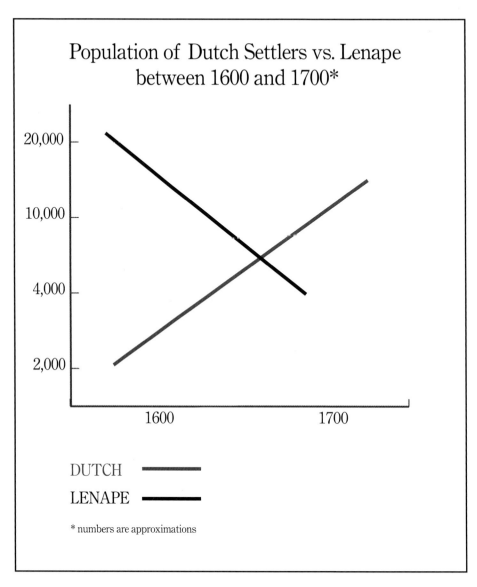

Population of Dutch Settlers vs. Lenape between 1600 and 1700*

DUTCH ━━━━

LENAPE ━━━━

* numbers are approximations

This graph shows the comparison between populations of Dutch settlers to the Lenape. The Lenape population dropped drastically in the years following contact with the settlers. It is important to understand that these numbers are just approximations since statistics such as these were not officially recorded at that time.

4. The Story of the Twenty-Four Dollar Purchase

Before Peter Stuyvesant arrived in New Amsterdam, there were other people whose actions and decisions played a key role in the founding and shaping of New Netherland. One of these was the former Director-General Peter Minuit. Minuit arrived in New Netherland on May 4, 1626. He was hired by the Dutch West India Company to replace the first director-general, Willem Verhulst, who arrived in 1625.

When the Dutch West India Company appointed Verhulst as leader of the colony and sent him to America, they gave him

Peter Minuit, a Walloon, was born in Wesel, Germany, in 1580.

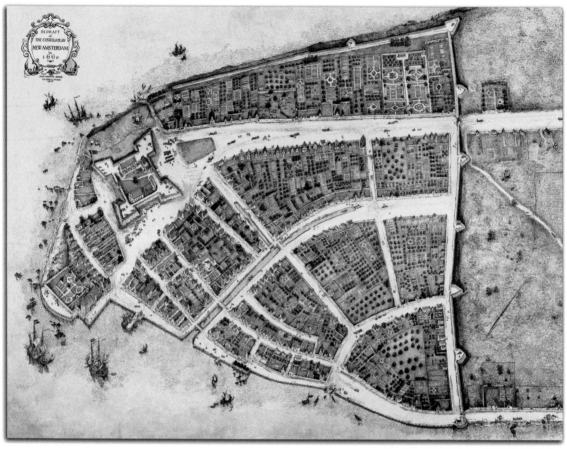

This redraft of the Costello Plan, showing New Amsterdam in 1660, was done by John Wolcott Adams and published by I.N. Phelps Stokes in 1916. The map shows the layout of the town in 1660. Note the position of the four-pointed fort at the tip of Manhattan, as well as the "Broad Way" that empties out right by the fort. The pier, on the bottom left in this picture, is also visible. Minuit chose Manhattan because its location on the water made it easy for trade ships and supplies to reach the Dutch inhabitants.

specific instructions about how to conduct company business. These instructions suggested where new families should settle in the colony and how to handle business with the Indians. The instructions were particularly specific about one thing. The employees of the Dutch West India Company were not to get involved in relations between native groups. The Company expected Verhulst to make sure employees followed these instructions.

One employee, however, disobeyed orders by interfering with Indian affairs. His name was Daniel Van Crieckenbeeck, and he was the commander of Fort Orange at present-day Albany. In 1626, Van Crieckenbeeck sided with the Mahican Indians in their war with the Mohawks. In this battle, he and three of his soldiers were killed. The colony fell into a panic. The Company blamed Verhulst for this trouble. They questioned whether Verhulst was a good leader because he was not enforcing their rules. Since he was not doing a good job, the Company removed him, and hired Peter Minuit to lead the colony.

After the incident with Van Crieckenbeeck, the Company was eager to prevent more conflicts with the Indians. Peter Minuit's first instruction from the Company was to gather the Dutch colonists scattered in different areas and bring them together in one place for safety. Minuit chose Manhattan Island. Surrounded by water, the island was fairly safe from attack and large enough to support the growing colony.

There is a popular story about how Peter Minuit bought Manhattan Island from the Lenape Indians for twenty-four dollars worth of beads and trinkets. Some

This 1939 oil painting by an unidentified artist shows the purchase of Manhattan Island by Peter Minuit.

versions of the story even give an exact date and location for the purchase. This legendary story of one of the best deals ever made is written about in books, illustrated in paintings, and even appears in songs and advertisements. Like many stories that have been told over time, however, it has been exaggerated, and details have been added for which there is no historical evidence.

The story of Peter Minuit and the twenty-four dollar purchase of Manhattan began to emerge in the mid-1800s, when a rare document was discovered in the Netherlands. In 1839, John Brodhead, secretary to a Dutch ambassador, found a letter in the royal archives. The letter was written in 1626 by a Dutch delegate, Peter Schagen, to his superiors in the Dutch government. Schagen was reporting about the status of the colony of New Netherland. The letter gave details of life and trade in New Amsterdam. Schagen also mentioned Manhattan: "They have purchased the Island Manhattes from the Indians for the value of sixty guilders."

This sentence from a single letter is the only evidence historians have about the purchase of Manhattan. The letter

Peter Schagen's letter gives a general status report for the settlement of New Amsterdam. He comments on the settlers well-being, their trade, and the prosperity of their farms: "...Yesterday the ship the Arms of Amsterdam arrived here. It sailed from New Netherland out of the River of Mauritius on the 23rd of September. They report that our people are in good spirit and live in peace. The women also have borne some children there. They have purchased the Island Manhattes from the Indians for the value of 60 guilders. It is 11,000 morgens in size [about 22,000 acres]. They had all their grain sowed by the middle of May, and reaped by the middle of August. They sent samples of these summer grains: wheat, rye, barley, oats, buckwheat, canary seed, beans, and flax.... Your High and Mightinesses' Obedient, P. Schagen."

itself is dated November 1626, but it does not say on what day the purchase took place. Nor does it say where the deal was made. It could have been anywhere on Manhattan Island or in the surrounding areas. The letter does not say that Peter Minuit bought Manhattan. Based on other evidence, historians generally agree that because it was Minuit who chose Manhattan, it was most likely he who conducted the purchase with the Lenape.

The letter also does not mention anything about twenty-four dollars. In fact there were no dollars in 1626. The United States was not yet an independent country with currency. The letter does mention the number sixty guilders, though. Guilders are Dutch money. So how did sixty guilders become the twenty-four dollars of the story? About the time the Schagen letter was discovered, it is believed that someone unknown to historians figured out that sixty guilders were worth about twenty-four dollars, and the number became part of the story.

The letter also makes no mention of what goods were traded for the island. However, other documents written in the 1600s that have survived today list the kinds of objects typically used in trade. The objects traded for Manhattan Island probably included such European-made items as brass kettles, copper pots, iron knives, axes, and cloth. Wampum and European glass beads may also have been included. Wampum are shell beads made by the Indians of the Northeast, who strung them together or fashioned them into belts. The Indians valued wampum and often used it as decoration, in trade, for gift giving, and for ceremonial occasions. Glass beads were also valued, but metal tools and utensils were worth far more. Not only were metal objects new and unusual,

Brass kettles like this one would have been a typical and valuable item received in trade by the Native Americans from the Dutch.

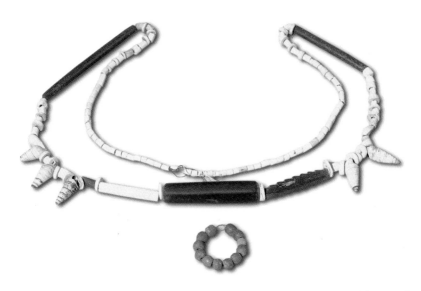

Photo courtesy of the Rochester Museum and Science Center, Rochester, New York

This picture shows the difference between European glass beads and Native American beads made from shell and stone. The blue beads above are glass beads, and the necklace was made by Indians from shell and catlinite beads.

Wampum is sometimes called Indian money, but money was not part of Indian culture. It was the colonists of New Netherland who used wampum as money when they began to run out of their own Dutch coins.

they were durable and lasted longer than Indian tools made of stone and bone, and pots made of clay. European cloth was also useful because it was ready for sewing. It did not have to be softened first, as did animal hides. These European-made objects would have been valuable to the Lenape, far more than the worthless trinkets mentioned in the story.

The story of Peter Minuit and his purchase of Manhattan is inaccurate in yet another way. It only tells one side of the story. The native peoples did not keep written records like the Europeans, so the story has been recorded only from the Dutch point of view. According to the Dutch, Manhattan Island was indeed purchased.

According to the Lenape, that would not have been the case. The Lenape did not believe that land could be owned, only that it could be shared. For them, accepting gifts from the

This metal axe head was a typical item that the Dutch might have used in trade with the Indians.

Dutch meant giving the Dutch the right to use the land, not own it.

Historians may never know all the details of the story of Peter Minuit and the purchase of Manhattan. All that is known for sure is that the Dutch West India Company acquired the island from the Lenape and it became the center of activity for the colony of New Netherland and for Peter Stuyvesant.

5. The Making of a Leader

Little is known about Peter Stuyvesant's childhood. Historians are even confused about the year of his birth. Some believe it was 1592, and others say it was 1602 or 1610. Stuyvesant was born in the town of Weststellingwerf in the Netherlands and raised in the province of Friesland. His parents were Balthazar Johannes Stuyvesant, a Dutch Reformed minister, and Margaretts Hardenstein. Together they raised Peter and his sister Anna under the strict laws of the Dutch Reformed Church, which were based on a strong devotion to God. The family lived in Scherpenzeel until moving to Berlicum in 1622. In 1625, Peter's mother died, and his father remarried in 1627. Through this second marriage, Peter and Anna now had two stepbrothers and two stepsisters.

Education was as important as religion in the Stuyvesant household. Peter attended school all through his youth. He applied himself and became fluent in Latin. In 1630, Peter began to study at the University of Franeker, where his father had graduated. But student life could not satisfy Peter's bold and courageous character. He was ready for adventure and a challenging career. He left the University and entered the Dutch military. He served his country both at home and abroad, satisfying his thirst for the wind, sea, and ships. He also developed the skills of an organized and disciplined soldier.

His achievement in the military led him to seek a position with the Dutch West India Company as an officer in charge of the Company's equipment and supplies in Brazil. He was so successful in this role that the Company recognized his commitment and dedication. In 1643, the Company promoted him to governor of the Dutch islands of Curaçao, Aruba, and Bonaire in the Caribbean, where the Company operated trade outposts. The islands produced an abundance of salt, sugar, rum, and indigo. These were highly valued goods in Europe and New Amsterdam. Here his job was to check and report on the cargo of ships and to have the goods delivered to Amsterdam. He even sought out captured ships with stolen cargo, and Dutch ships by-passing the Dutch West India Company by sailing under the British flag! This was a responsible assignment for the young Peter, which brought him a sizable increase in salary.

The Dutch were not the only European forces competing for the rich trade goods in the Caribbean. The Spanish and the French also had powerful

This modern day picture of Willemstad, Curaçao shows the Curaçao Trading Company. It was companies like this one that Peter Stuyvesant would have managed when he was governor. You can still see the Dutch influence in the gabled windows on the buildings.

outposts. The Spanish in particular posed a threat to the Dutch West India Company in the Caribbean because of the strained relationship between the Dutch and the Spanish in Europe. This tension threatened the Company's potential to expand their business.

Peter's military background prepared him to act as commander of the islands, and he led numerous attacks against the Spanish. The most famous of these was the 1644 assault on a Spanish fort on the island of St.

Martin. This island had excellent salt beds and tobacco. Peter was determined to claim the island for the Dutch, before the British or the French tried to capture the fort for themselves. In a letter to the directors in Amsterdam, Peter and his council wrote that "if this occupation by the English or French occurs before us, then the Company would suffer considerable damage from the duties and claims to other salt throughout the Indies, because the saltpans of the island of St. Martyn [St. Martin] are more accessible than any other region and for this reason the ships from the fatherland as well as elsewhere would prefer to seek a cargo there than elsewhere; in addition because the aforesaid island is located in the proximity of the Caribbean's population...they can expect some prizes, which will not only damage the Company but lead to the detriment of the general trade of our fatherland."

Early in the siege, a cannonball struck Peter in his right leg, forcing him to return to Curaçao. His injury was so severe that his leg needed to be amputated below the knee. In the tropical climate, Peter's amputated leg

---

The map on the next two pages was created around 1540 by Giovanni Battista Agnese. It shows the routes by which trade ships carried goods around the world. These routes were chosen based on the favorable trade winds large sailing vessels needed. European ships sailing to Asia brought back spices and silks. The Caribbean supplied salt, sugar, rum, and indigo, which were brought into New Netherland and traded for beaver fur. The fur, along with the lumber, was then brought back to Europe for trade. In exchange, Europe supplied metal and glass objects to trade with the Indians. This created a diverse market of goods in the 1600s.

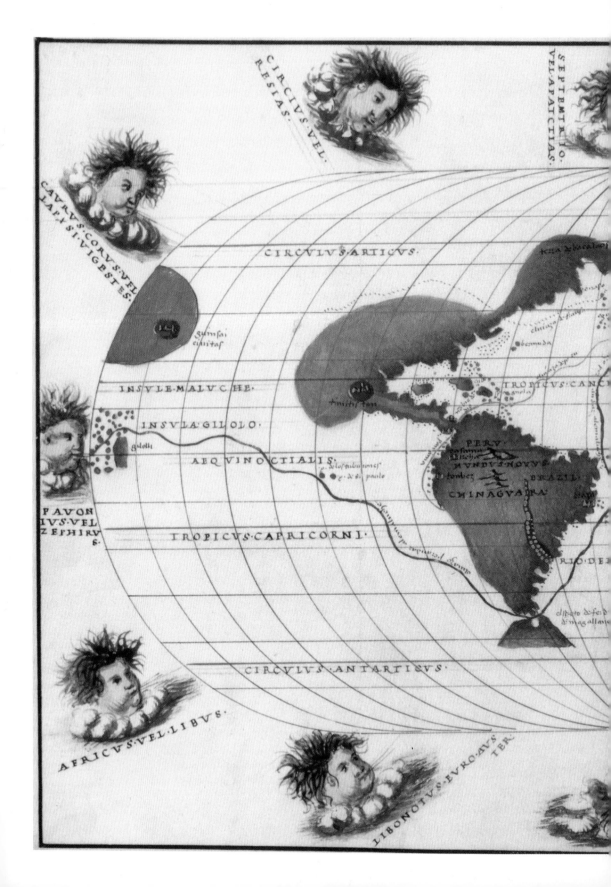

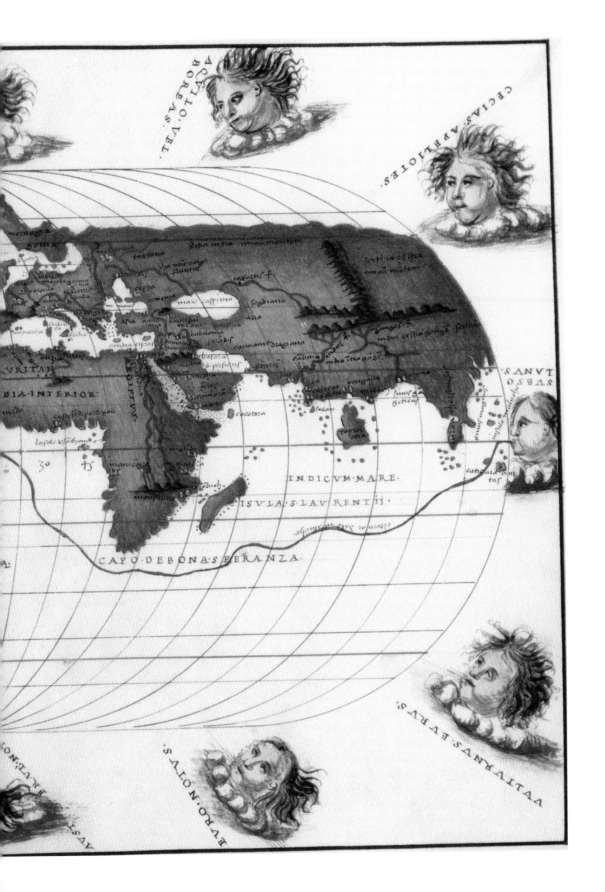

did not heal properly and he was required to return to the Netherlands to recuperate. Peter felt miserable about returning home. He was determined to serve the Company, and he did not want to leave during this crucial time. What good could he do lying in a bed? But his wound was causing him terrible pain.

In the Netherlands he was fitted with an artificial leg. His new leg was decorated with silver bands, so it was often referred to as his "silver leg." Most likely his artificial leg was made of wood, which would have made standing extremely uncomfortable. Since there were no painkillers in the 1600s, Peter probably spent most of his life dealing with a throbbing pain.

Luckily for Peter, this period of recuperation in

© Collection of the New-York Historical Society/1858.28

This detail from "Peter Stuyvesant and the Trumpeter" (see page 11) shows Stuyvesant's wooden leg.

the Netherlands did not threaten his career. His determination enabled him to maintain his status with the Company. Finally in 1645, when Peter was well enough, the Dutch West India Company approved his return to the Americas as director-general of New Netherland and the Dutch Caribbean islands. This was the high point of his career, and a position he had worked very hard to achieve. He welcomed the opportunity and took his advancement seriously.

Despite how it seemed, life was not all work for Peter. On August 13, 1645, he married Judith Bayard. Peter and Judith were married at the Walloon Church of Breda, where Judith's father had served as a minister. He had probably gotten to know Judith through his sister Anna, who was married to Judith's brother, Samuel Bayard. Within a year of his marriage, Peter took his oath of office as director-general of New Netherland in July 1646.

On Christmas day in 1646, the couple boarded the *Great Crow* along with Judith's widowed sister, her four children, and members of

This is a portrait of Peter Stuyvesant's sister, Anna Merica Bayard.

This is a woodcut of the landing of the Dutch settlers on Manhattan Island. The Dutch West India Company sent two main groups to settle in New Netherland, the first in 1624, the second in 1626. This picture probably does not show the first European group to land on Manhattan because there are already buildings here. Peter Stuyvesant probably arrived in a similar setting, but by the time he arrived in 1647, the area would have been even more populated.

Peter's new staff. Peter first instructed the crew to sail to Curaçao, in the Dutch Caribbean, and then up the Atlantic Coast to New Netherland. They docked in their new home, New Amsterdam, on May 11, 1647. It is here that the disciplined Peter would leave an impression on the colonists that would be his legacy.

6. New Netherland's New Leader

Stuyvesant was eager to begin his post as director-general of New Netherland, and he wanted everyone to be aware of his new rank. On his way to New Amsterdam, where his headquarters were located, he directed his ship to travel into the Dutch Caribbean and stop in Curaçao, his former place of business. Here he was able to publicize personally his new role and let the colonists and employees of the Company know he intended to run a tight business both in the Caribbean as well as New Netherland. The stop in Curaçao set the tone for how he would begin the most important position of his career.

Although Stuyvesant was director-general of all New Netherland, the colonists of New Amsterdam, the busiest, and most populated of all the Company outposts, awaited Stuyvesant's arrival with great anticipation. The affairs in New Amsterdam would demand most of his attention. The colonists had heard stories of this great leader and how he had led the Company's efforts in the Caribbean. They expected

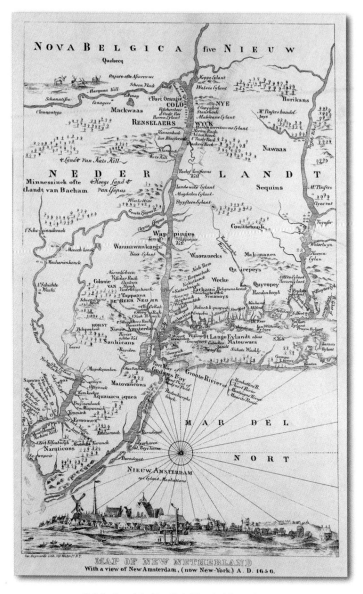

This is a lithograph by George Haywards of a map and drawing of New Netherland originally created by Adriaen van der Donck. Van der Donck's map was thought to date to 1656. Recent evidence suggests, however, that the original map and drawing were actually created by van der Donck, a member of Stuyvesant's council of nine, in 1648 to illustrate his *Remonstrance* (see page 63). The original was found in 1991, and apears to have served as a basis for many later drawings of New Amsterdam, including an etching on a map done by Claes Janzoon Visscher in 1650.

Stuyvesant to organize their quickly growing town, which would help to increase their wealth and prosperity.

New Amsterdam, at the tip of Manhattan, would become the colony's capital because of the geography of the harbor that surrounded it. The harbor was deep and close to the Atlantic Ocean, making it easy for large boats to reach the city. The harbor also connected to the North River (present-day Hudson) that went deep into the interior. As ships entered the harbor, the first thing they saw was New Amsterdam's enormous windmill towering over the gabled rooftops. It looked like a town in the Netherlands, and the Europeans who came to work there immediately felt at home.

The town bustled with activity. Many docks lined the shore and were busy with ships bringing goods such as indigo, rum, sugar, and salt from the Caribbean and silks and spices from

© Collection of the New-York Historical Society/1945.519a-c

This Delft tile, probably created between 1750–1800, shows a windmill. Delft tiles such as this were commonly used in the Netherlands as well as in New Netherland in the 1600s. This tile shows a windmill similar to the one central to New Amsterdam's life and geography.

This is an illustration of ships in the harbor of New Amsterdam in 1667.

Asia. The seamen unloaded the ships and traded the goods with the Indians and colonists. Once the ships were unloaded, they were packed full of beaver and other furs received in trade from the Indians, who were eager for European goods. The Dutch West India Company ran the colony, so trade was only supposed to be conducted on its behalf. It was easy, however, to conduct private business, too, despite the Company's laws against it. The colonists quickly became accustomed to private profit.

Ships carried merchants from around the world, and

they brought news from far away places. Not only were the stories interesting, but they could be heard in eighteen different languages! The town was as diverse as it was busy. Colonists, traders, and seamen lined the crooked streets of New Amsterdam and engaged in business and gossip. A day's work often led to socializing in the local taverns where laughter and talk filled the air. Taverns were so central to the community that in 1641, the Stadt Herbergh, or City Tavern, was made the town hall. In fact, drinking and tavern life in New Amsterdam were so popular that by 1648 a

BANKING · BARTERING AND SHIPPING IN NEW AMSTERDAM 1650·

Banking, bartering, and shipping in New Amsterdam.
This painting shows the bustling life in the streets of New Amsterdam. Ships were constantly arriving to pick up furs and drop off goods for trade. Indians and merchants bartered for goods. The livelihood of the colony was centered around how busy and prosperous its trade was.

This painting showing the interior of a tavern was created by Willem van Herp between 1614-1677. The tavern served as the center of the community for the Dutch colony. Whole families could be found there relaxing or listening to news from across the ocean.

quarter of the houses in the city were taverns!

Beer was a staple drink in the 1600s, even for children. The Dutch West India Company imported seeds to grow wheat and erected a brewery so the colonists could enjoy their usual beverage. The windmill was close to the brewery because it also needed wheat to produce the flour for the food basics of the 1600s, such as pretzels, waffles, cookies, and pancakes. These baked goods were also popular trade items with the Indians, who were unfamiliar with European foods. The Dutch introduced both brewing and milling to New Netherland. The Company even sent over cows so the colonists could enjoy butter, milk, and cheese.

While everyone was busy trading and enjoying tavern life, the town fell into disrepair. Buildings were not kept up, the streets were not maintained and residents were not mindful of their pigs and cows. When the disciplined and regimented Stuyvesant arrived, he did not approve of the colony's condition, or how it was operating. He considered the colony, which had deteriorated under former Director-General Willem Kieft, disorganized. He wrote of the fort:

© Collection of the New-York Historical Society/1937.1313ab

These ice skates were made between 1825–75 out of wood, iron, leather, and fiber. Skates in the 1600s would have been similar to these.

Water bordered much of the Netherlands, so ice-skating became a popular winter sport. When the Dutch moved to New Netherland, they brought this well-liked activity with them.

"Whereas the fortress New Amsterdam is now and for sometime past...greatly decayed, and the walls daily leaped over and more and more trodden underfoot by men and cattle." He found that not only was the fort rundown, so were the many houses in which the town's seven hundred people lived. People threw their garbage into the dirt streets, relying on the livestock that roamed the town to "collect" it. Stuyvesant was also disturbed to find that many of the townspeople were drunkards. Brawls and knife fights were common, and tipsy men drove wagons and carts recklessly through the streets.

Stuyvesant moved swiftly through the town, despite his wooden leg, and immediately sought to improve the town's appearance. The colonists, who were accustomed to useless and unskilled leaders like Kieft, were ready for a capable director. They didn't realize how far Stuyvesant would go to establish order. He banned pigpens and outhouses from the streets and insisted on fences to keep animals in. He ordered that taverns close at 9 P.M., instead of their usual 10 P.M., and imposed stiff penalties on those who brawled or fought with knives. Stuyvesant increased the number of sermons preached on Sundays, and prohibited all business, social activity, and drinking on that day. He attempted to control smuggling and illegal business transactions by inspecting all ships and reviewing the account books. Punishments were stern. He threatened heavy fines and the loss of business licenses.

This picture shows Peter Stuyvesant yelling at the citizens of New Amsterdam. Stuyvesant's gruff ways and strict rules were becoming customary to the people of New Amsterdam. The people surrounding Stuyvesant in this picture seem to be looking at him as a spectacle rather than a fearsome leader.

The colonists were outraged. They could not believe Stuyvesant would impose such strict rules. They understood his intention, but felt their independence

© Collection of the New-York Historical Society/1950.355

"Peter Stuyvesant and the Cobbler" was painted by John Whetton Ehninger in 1850. It is oil on canvas. The painting was based on Irving's A History of New York. Paintings like this helped to perpetuate the legend of Stuyvesant's harsh leadership over the people of New Amsterdam. In this painting, Ehninger mistakenly painted Stuyvesant's wooden leg on the left instead of the right.

was being threatened. So they complained to Stuyvesant's bosses at the Company. The Amsterdam Chamber, made up of nineteen men located in Amsterdam, controlled company policies and supervised Stuyvesant. Yet there was only so much they could do from across the ocean when it took months for news to travel back and forth. This proved helpful to Stuyvesant, who implemented changes for the colony with or without the support of his superiors.

One of the major complaints lodged with the Chamber was Adriaen van der Donck's *Remonstrance,* a document that detailed all the problems in New Netherland. In it he questioned the Dutch West India Company's ability to govern the colony, urged the removal of Stuyvesant, and gave a detailed report on the deplorable state of New Amsterdam. He wrote that the colony was "in ruinous condition" due to "bad government" and "the windmill is neglected and, in consequence of having had a leaky roof most of the time, has become considerably rotten, so that it cannot now go with more than two arms, and it has been so for nearly five years." He went on to say that "the fort under which we are to shelter ourselves, and from which as it seems all authority proceeds, lies like a molehill or a tottering wall, on which there is not one gun-carriage or one piece of cannon in a suitable frame, or on a good platform."

To be fair, though, Stuyvesant had lodged similar complaints of the deplorable conditions in New Amsterdam. Van der Donck wanted Peter Stuyvesant removed, but Stuyvesant had been hired to turn around this "ruinous" state of affairs. He wasn't going to stop just because the settlers did not like him. However his methods might have been viewed, he believed he was working in the colony's best interest.

7. Stuyvesant Takes Control

Stuyvesant thought that New Amsterdam faced horrendous problems. Yet with every improvement he made, the gap between the colonists and him widened. They considered him mean and bossy, but he viewed his work as indispensable. His directorship was torn between his love for the colony and the will of the people. To help with important company decisions, Stuyvesant created a city council of nine. He appointed eighteen men, and from these the people of the town elected the nine. Unfortunately, the relationship between the nine council members and Peter Stuyvesant often proved more tense than productive.

This was Director-General Peter Stuyvesant's seal.

The first difficult test faced by Stuyvesant, his council of nine, and the colonists began within three weeks of Stuyvesant's arrival. Cornelis Melyn and Joachim Pietersen Kuyter had written a letter of complaint to the Amsterdam Chamber. The letter said that under Director-General Kieft their property had been destroyed by fire in an Indian attack. Kieft was already in the process of being replaced by Stuyvesant. The two men feared that once Kieft returned to Amsterdam, the havoc he had permitted in the community would be forgotten and they would never be repaid for the property they lost. Once Stuyvesant arrived in New Amsterdam, Melyn and Kuyter drew up charges against Kieft. This put Stuyvesant in a position of either supporting Kieft or the colonists. To make matters worse, Kieft then charged the men with rebellious and disloyal behavior towards him and the Dutch West India Company. Stuyvesant was annoyed. He felt that the Melyn and Kuyter affair was a silly distraction, and that there were more important issues at hand. Yet he decided that he would show the colonists he meant to rule with a firm hand, and put the two men on trial. At first he ordered a death sentence, but his council of nine passionately disagreed. Finally, the two men were banished from the colony.

The Melyn and Kuyter affair did not get Stuyvesant's administration off to an easy start. The colonists now viewed him as a "company" man, and not one who would uphold their rights. Stuyvesant could not worry about that. His main concern was to attend to the colony's more immediate problems. It was falling apart! He continued to put into place ordinances that boosted the town's appearance and well-being. He ordered drivers to get out of their wagons and lead their horses through town. This slowed down traffic and made it safe to walk. The only street where drivers could ride in their wagons was Broadway, but they had to obey a low speed limit. He put

This painting by Thomas Hill shows Broadway in 1636. Broadway was the only street in New Amsterdam where men could ride their carriages and horses through the town. Broadway is still in existence in modern-day New York City.

This undated engraving of three houses and a church shows the beginning of a Dutch settlement. The artist is unknown.

into place measures that protected the town from fire, which was the greatest hazard during colonial times. One spark from a chimney could set the town afire. He helped formulate a fire code requiring people to keep their chimneys clean and their homes fireproof. He appointed wardens to enforce the code and fine violators. He also organized the colony's first "rattle watch," nine men who patrolled the streets between tavern closing time and six in the morning, watching over the colony by night. Stuyvesant ordered repairs on the fort, completed construction of a Dutch Reformed church, directed the building of paved streets, arranged for garbage to be carted away, and maintained the ports along the shoreline.

All these improvements cost money, so Stuyvesant began to tax the colonists. He imposed the first tax on wines and liquors within his first two months. This furthered the divide between him and the colonists. Stuyvesant knew he also had to keep a watchful eye on the Company's business and stop illegal trading. The closer he watched, the more laws he made. He especially watched the business of the bakers in the town. He established weight and price control on bread, and required that white bread and cakes be baked for personal consumption only, not for trade.

The colonists began to stop taking him seriously, laughing at each new ordinance read aloud in the Town Square. If this wasn't enough for Stuyvesant, he also had to worry that his colony would be taken over by the English, whose settlements surrounded New Netherland.

With all this responsibility, Stuyvesant barely had time for his family. Judith bore two sons in New Amsterdam, Balthazar Lazarus in 1647 and Nicholas William a year later. Stuyvesant's boys, like him, were schooled and raised in a strict Dutch Reformed home. The boys enjoyed the security that their father had

This engraving shows Peter Stuyvesant's home,
"The Whitehall" in 1658.

helped to create in New Amsterdam and lived
comfortably in Whitehall, the spacious home the family
built on land purchased from the Company. They called
the property the Great Bouwery, after the Dutch word
for farm. Later enlarged by more land purchases, the
farm ran from the East River to what is now Fourth
Avenue and Broadway. The road that led from New

Amsterdam to his house is still called the Bouwery (today spelled Bowery). Stuyvesant paid 6,400 guilders for the land, a house, a barn, six cows, two horses, and two young African slaves. Due to the importance of religion in his life, he built a private chapel to bring him peace and quiet from the colonists. Stuyvesant loved his farm and found great serenity there.

In his quest to control New Netherland, Stuyvesant strove to make the colony religious. However, the only religion Stuyvesant acknowledged was his own, Dutch Reformed. Despite the ethnic diversity of New Amsterdam by 1660, he believed everyone should worship like he did. He banned all public and private

The Jews who came to New Amsterdam in 1654 were from the Dutch colonies in Brazil. After the Netherlands turned Brazil over to the Portuguese, the Jews were forced to flee persecution. In New Amsterdam they founded the congregation Shearith Israel. Today, this is the oldest Jewish congregation in North America.

religious meetings, including those of the Quakers and Lutherans.

In 1654, twenty-four Sephardic Jews arrived in New Amsterdam from the Dutch colonies in Brazil that had been recently conquered by the Portuguese. Stuyvesant did not hide his displeasure. The Jews arrived exhausted after their long journey. In order to pay for their voyage, they had to auction their belongings, reducing them to poverty. In Stuyvesant's view, the colony had enough problems already. How could he take care of these homeless people? Stuyvesant stripped the Jews of any personal rights, including owning land and businesses, but they quickly complained to the Amsterdam Chamber. The Chamber required Stuyvesant to permit these basic freedoms to the Jews, who eventually prospered.

Like the Jews, the Quakers also suffered under Stuyvesant's rule. In 1657, two Quaker women began preaching in the streets of New Amsterdam. Stuyvesant first jailed them, then banished them from the colony. To protest Stuyvesant's cruelty, Quakers in the town of Flushing began to hold their services openly, instead of in secret. Stuyvesant arrested several of them. In response the people of Flushing wrote a letter, known as the Flushing Remonstrance, asking for basic, individual rights. The Chamber in Amsterdam read the letter and told Stuyvesant to mend his ways. It supported people of all different backgrounds who wished to live and work in New Netherland. The Company was solely interested in keeping employees and making money. Religious beliefs were not their concern.

Stuyvesant was troubled. He had always been committed to instilling religious virtue among the people. From the start of his administration he had taken a leading role in the education of New Netherland's children. Boys and girls, European and African, were taught reading and writing along with lessons from the Dutch Reformed Church. Stuyvesant felt that his religion held the answers, and never agreed with the Chamber in allowing diversity in the colony. This issue would never be settled between Stuyvesant and the Company. As in his relationship with the colonists, Stuyvesant stood alone in his ideas.

8. Threats of Takeover

Peter Stuyvesant's challenges as a leader included more than squabbles with the people of New Netherland. While trying to keep peace among his own people, Stuyvesant also had to protect them, and to keep New Netherland from being taken over by the larger English colonies nearby. These included New England to the north and the English colony of Virginia to the south. New Netherland was valuable, with its rich farmland and open waterways, and the English were moving gradually into the land claimed by the Dutch.

New Netherland was begun for trading purposes, not as a permanent settlement. Therefore, when New Netherland was first established, the Dutch West India Company did not fix boundaries for the fledgling colony. However, the Dutch West India Company did not want to lose its business enterprise to the English settlers, who had come to build a new life in America.

Surrounded on all sides by the English, Stuyvesant knew that his colony was at risk. He also knew that

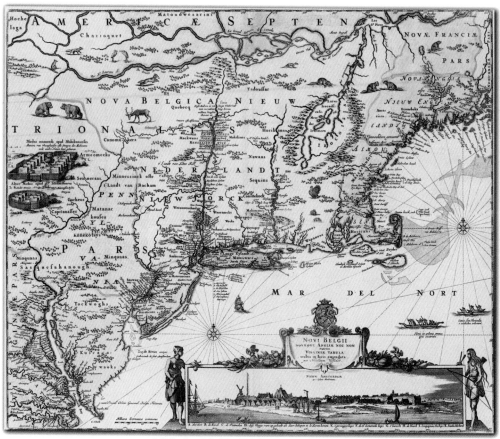

This map of America's eastern seaboard is believed to have been created by Claes Janszoon Visscher sometime around 1651. It is also believed that the inset of New Amsterdam was based on the van der Donck map of 1648 (see page 54). Unlike the van der Donck view, however, Visscher's map represents a nicer, more "promotional" view of the city, in order to encourage people to settle in New Netherland.

without proper boundaries it would be difficult for the Dutch to keep the English out. In 1650, he went to Hartford, the capital of the Connecticut colony, to discuss the issue of land rights and borders with New England officials. During this meeting, Stuyvesant had to make certain choices in negotiating with New England. Although he wanted to keep all of Long Island Dutch, he had to give up some lands in order to keep others, especially those areas that had access to the Hudson and to the Atlantic for shipping and transportation.

The meeting between Stuyvesant and the New England officials resulted in an agreement known as the Treaty of Hartford. Long Island would be divided at the town of Oyster Bay. The Dutch would have the land west of Oyster Bay south to the Atlantic Ocean, while the land to the east would belong to the English. In Connecticut the boundary would be drawn between Greenwich and Stamford. Greenwich would be Dutch and Stamford English. Hartford would remain under English rule, but the Dutch would be allowed to keep a fort there. The Treaty of Hartford also called for friendly relations between the English and Dutch people in case they ever had to unite against a common enemy.

Not long after the Treaty of Hartford was signed, something happened in Europe that was to pose a serious threat to the Dutch holdings in New Netherland. War broke out between England and the Netherlands over the Navigation Act passed by the English Parliament in 1651. The Act said that European goods entering England could only be brought by English ships or the ships of the country where the goods were made. Non-European goods could

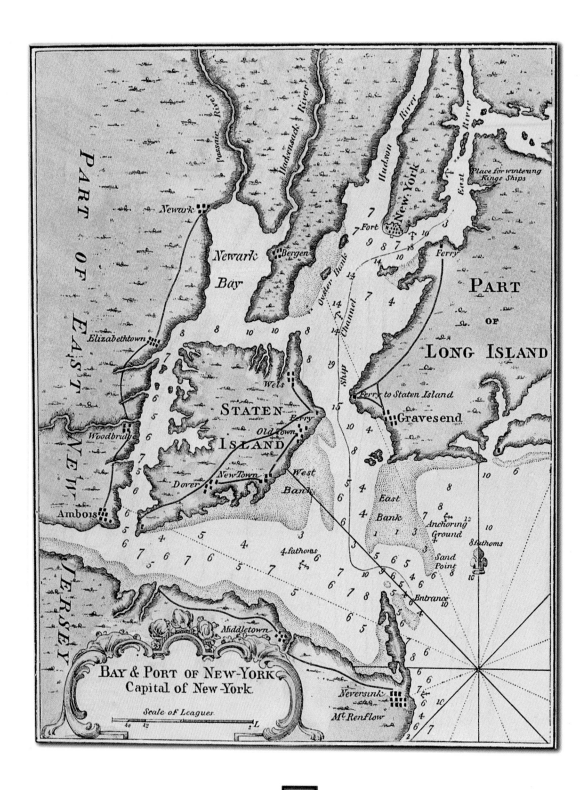

Clashes between the British and the Dutch, such as the one spurred by the Navigation Act of 1651, became known as the Anglo-Dutch Wars. There were three Anglo-Dutch Wars between 1652 and 1674, all related to conflicts over trading rights and land ownership.

only be brought by English ships. Both England and the Netherlands were leaders in world trade. By passing the Navigation Act, England put limitations on Dutch business. The two countries went to war.

Although this war took place in Europe, it provided a good excuse for the English in America to take over New Netherland. The English felt they no longer had to respect the Treaty of Hartford and freely crossed the boundaries. To make matters worse, many Englishmen

Opposite: S. Bellin's rare map of the New York City area was created in 1764. It is a hand-colored woodcut. Although this map was drawn after Peter Stuyvesant's time, it is still an excellent view of the land that was owned by New Netherland in the 1600s. New Amsterdam was an attractive piece of property, because of its location. Stuyvesant was aware of this and took steps to fortify the town against attack.

living in the Dutch areas of Long Island, who once had an allegiance to Stuyvesant, now rebelled against Dutch rule and sided with New England.

As reports of the war in Europe reached New Amsterdam by ship, other reports came to Stuyvesant that New England was beginning to prepare for war against New Netherland. When Stuyvesant heard the news, he started making plans for the city of New Amsterdam to defend itself. In March 1653, he called a meeting with city officials to discuss what could be done. They decided to order a guard to stand watch each night at City Hall. They also ordered Jan Jansen Vischer, skipper of a ship that had just entered port, to load the cannon on his vessel and keep the ship ready in case of emergency. The fort at New Amsterdam was in terrible condition, so they ordered it repaired and strengthened. The fort itself was not big enough to hold all the people of New Amsterdam in case of attack. Money was raised among citizens to build a high stockade around the exposed areas of the city, which included the northern end. Today the street running along the line where this northern wall was built is still called Wall Street, one of New York's most famous thoroughfares.

While Stuyvesant and the people of New Amsterdam were preparing their defenses, rumors reached New England about what Stuyvesant was doing. The reports in New England were exaggerated, as if Stuyvesant was about to wage war against the English

Augustine Herrman created this engraving of New Amsterdam in the mid-1600s.

colony. The reports also falsely claimed Stuyvesant was encouraging the Indians to get involved. When Stuyvesant heard of these false reports, he offered to meet with representatives from New England. New England accepted Stuyvesant's offer and sent three men to Manhattan to meet with Stuyvesant. Many people thought the men were really sent to spy on Stuyvesant to see what was going on in New Amsterdam, because they left quickly without discussing much.

In February 1654, the English general Oliver Cromwell sent a letter to New England urging colonists to take over New Netherland. Cromwell said he was sending men, ships, and weapons for that purpose,

This portrait of Oliver Cromwell was painted by Flemish painter Gaspar de Crayer between 1584–1669. During the first civil war in England, Cromwell rose rapidly because of his military ability and genius for organization. In 1653, Cromwell dissolved the Rump Parliament and replaced it with the Nominated, or Barebone's, Parliament. That same year the Protectorate was established and Cromwell was named lord protector. Cromwell's foreign policy was governed by the need to expand English trade and prevent the return of the Stuarts to power. He approved the Navigation Act of 1651, which led to the first of the Anglo-Dutch Wars.

although he told his officials in New England not to be cruel to the Dutch colonists. They were to be allowed to stay under English rule or be given permission to go back to Europe. On May 12, the first of Cromwell's ships arrived in Boston. Others followed. Eventually they planned to sail to New Netherland and request surrender. Realizing that it was only a matter of time before his colony was invaded, Stuyvesant began to recruit an army.

Meanwhile, back in Europe, neither England nor the Netherlands was winning the war. The two countries called a truce, known as the Treaty of Westminster. It was signed in April, but news of it did not reach Stuyvesant until July 17. Fortunately for the people of New Netherland, the news of the treaty came to the New World before the English ships invaded their colony. Cromwell sent a letter to New England canceling the attack, and the English ships left the area. The people of New Amsterdam, having narrowly escaped a takeover, held a celebration.

9. Stuyvesant Continues to Battle

There were two other dangers to New Netherland besides the threat of war with New England. One was attack by the Indians of the region and the other was the establishment of a Swedish colony on Dutch land.

The colonists were concerned about their relationship with the Indians. Occasionally misunderstandings between the two resulted in colonists and Indians getting hurt or killed and property damaged. The worst of these incidents took place before Peter Stuyvesant's arrival, when former Director-General Willem Kieft tried to tax the Indians. This led to frequent skirmishes between the Dutch and the Indians, and a horrible massacre of the Indians in 1643. The Indians later sought revenge. Both Indians and colonists continued to battle one another until both sides called a truce in 1645. Some of the colonists still did not deal fairly with the Indians in trade and often tried to cheat them. The relationship between the Dutch and the Indians remained tense.

While the Indians posed a threat to life and

This painting shows the Indian Massacre by New Netherland director-general Kieft in the 1640s. Relations between the Indians and the Dutch were particularly violent under Kieft's leadership. Rather than negotiate with the Indians, he chose to try and intimidate them. After several incidents, Kieft decided to make an example of the Wecquaesgeek tribe and launched a surprise attack that killed more than one hundred Indians. This led to the Wappinger War, between 1643 and 1645.

property, the Swedes were a threat to business. They had arrived on the Delaware River in 1638, sent by the Swedish South Company. Like New Netherland, New Sweden was established for the purpose of trading furs.

back. Meanwhile, Stuyvesant heard that there had been an Indian attack in Manhattan. He did not have time for Rising's stalling tactics, so he ordered Rising to surrender or be attacked. Rising surrendered on September 24. Stuyvesant allowed the Swedish soldiers to leave the fort with honors, marching out with banners to the music of fifes and drums. He then returned to Manhattan to deal with the problems there.

For the first eight years of his leadership, Stuyvesant had managed to keep peace between the Dutch and the Indians. While Stuyvesant was gone, however, the Mahican, Pachami, Esopus, and Hackensack Indians decided to attack their traditional enemies, the Indians of eastern Long Island. While on their way, the Indians stopped at Manhattan to rest and eat. One of the Indians started to pick peaches from a nearby orchard and was shot and killed by the Dutchman who owned the orchard. This set off a chain of events, called the Peach War, that resulted in many people, both Dutch and Indian, being captured and killed. Much property was also damaged.

Stuyvesant returned to a city full of fear and panic, and he immediately took action to calm the people. He ordered all ships to remain anchored for the city's protection, and all men on board had to stay there in

Opposite: Johan Rising, the Swedish colonial governor of New Sweden, is on a boat on the Delaware River.

case they were needed to fight. He also ordered that a new wall of planks be built around the city because he didn't think the existing one was tall enough. Residents of the city were told they could not go into the countryside unless they traveled in large groups for safety. To provide security for the colonists in the countryside, Stuyvesant ordered that new farms had to be built close to one another. Finally, Stuyvesant made plans to meet with the Indian leaders to make a truce with them and ransom Dutch prisoners that had been taken.

Although Stuyvesant's efforts at peace were successful, other raids and wars occurred in 1659, and again in 1663. Again Stuyvesant negotiated with the Indian leaders and peace was restored.

Meanwhile Stuyvesant was still concerned about New England. Even though the immediate threat of war between the Dutch and English colonies had ceased, Stuyvesant still worried that New England wanted to take over New Netherland. He wrote to his superiors at the Amsterdam Chamber, telling them about his fears. The Chamber felt Stuyvesant's fears were unfounded. A few years earlier, in 1660, England had crowned a new king, Charles II, and the Dutch government was sure that this new king was friendly towards the Netherlands. When Stuyvesant wrote asking the Chamber to send more soldiers and supplies to New Amsterdam, the Chamber refused. Stuyvesant continued to write, insisting that the threat to New

Netherland was real, and the Chamber continued to ignore Stuyvesant's fears. Recognizing he would not get any help from his superiors in the Netherlands, Stuyvesant began to prepare the colony for attack. Guards were put on patrol day and night to watch the city, and the fort and city walls were strengthened.

Stuyvesant showed great wisdom in predicting that the English would try to take over New Netherland. In March 1664, King Charles gave a large portion of land in America to his brother James,

This is a portrait of Charles II, king of England.

the Duke of York. Part of that gift included New Netherland. Under the command of Colonel Richard Nicholls, James sent a fleet of warships to take possession of his new land. By August the English ships had positioned themselves around New Amsterdam, closing off the city. Soldiers had been

James, Duke of York, became king of England in 1685, but was forced to give up the throne in 1688. William of Orange, the ruler of the Netherlands became king in his place.

dropped off on land in Brooklyn, opposite the city, and more were coming from New England.

Peter Stuyvesant knew his colony was in danger. He had been receiving accounts from a man in Curaçao, Matthias Beck, of some suspicious activities by the British: "Among other things they also inform and warn me of hostile and untrustworthy actions of the English....They advise...three to four ships have arrived from England headed for New England...that your honors shall first come to suffer a strong attack at the Manhattans by the English neighbors." This letter probably arrived too late but it was not the first reference in letters between Stuyvesant and Beck of the possibility of attack from the British.

Nevertheless, when the attack came, Stuyvesant's soldiers were greatly outnumbered, and their supply of gunpowder and lead was low. Colonel Nicholls ordered Stuyvesant to surrender. Stuyvesant tried to negotiate,

The Second Anglo-Dutch War, lasting from 1664 through 1667, erupted over British seizure of Dutch posts in West Africa in 1663 and the capture of New Amsterdam in 1664. This painting by an unknown artist portrays a sea battle between England and Holland in June 1666. It was just one of many that occurred during the war.

but Nicholls refused. The situation looked hopeless for New Netherland. Although city officials urged Stuyvesant to surrender, he still hoped to find a way to save his colony. Finally, on September 5, the people of New Amsterdam sent their director-general a petition asking him to surrender. None of them wanted a war. Ninety-three of the city's men, including Stuyvesant's own son, Balthazar, signed the request. That afternoon Stuyvesant surrendered.

Peter Stuyvesant tears up the summons to surrender New Amsterdam to the British in 1664. Stuyvesant desperately wanted to keep his colony from the British, but he was outnumbered and the Dutch settlers did not want a war.

"The Fall of New Amsterdam, 1664" was painted by Jean Leon Gerome Ferris. Stuyvesant reluctantly surrendered New Amsterdam to the British on September 5, 1664. The terms of surrender were extremely lenient for the times. The Dutch were allowed to keep their property, citizenship, and most of the freedoms they had enjoyed under Dutch rule.

On September 8, 1664, New Amsterdam was renamed New York in honor of James, Duke of York. The terms of surrender were extremely lenient, so life for the Dutch did not change much under English rule. The English allowed the Dutch to keep their property and continue their laws and customs. While some of the Dutch chose to return to Europe, most remained, including Stuyvesant and his family.

St. Nicholas Day, celebrated on December 5th, was a popular Dutch holiday. The Dutch name for St. Nick, patron of children, was Sinter Klaus. Before going to bed on the eve of the 5th, children would place their shoes by the fireside in hopes that St. Nick would fill them with plums and sugar treats. Once New Amsterdam became New York, the Dutch continued this tradition in the English colony. However, the Dutch name Sinter Klaus became the English Santa Claus.

10. The Dutch Legacy

Peter Stuyvesant remained committed to New Netherland throughout his period of leadership, despite his differences with the Amsterdam Chamber, his council of nine, and the colonists. It was a sad day for him when the Dutch colonial empire fell into English hands, only forty years after it began. However, the influence of the short Dutch period on the growth of New York City has been long lasting. As in the days of beaver skins and wampum, New York is still a place of commerce. Lower Manhattan, where New Amsterdam was centered and where the wall marked the town's northernmost boundary, is still considered the center of business.

Although Stuyvesant wanted a Dutch Reformed colony, the desire of the Amsterdam Chamber to create a city of tolerance and diversity has prevailed. New York City today is still multicultural and varied, as it was in the 1600s. The city welcomes people from all backgrounds and offers opportunity for economic success.

Little remains of the town of New Amsterdam. No

The Stock Exchange on Wall Street today in New York City.

mills or bakers' quarters survive. Only the crooked streets of the original New Amsterdam remain! The same street layout, designed in the early 1600s, is still the pattern today, and these streets have names that call to mind the city's Dutch colonial past. Beaver Street calls to mind the city's dependence on the beaver trade, while Stone Street was the first cobbled street in New Amsterdam. Pearl Street was once piled high with oyster shells and Water Street marks the place where the shoreline once began. Of course New York's most famous thoroughfare is Broadway, the "broad way" which ran through the middle of old New Amsterdam.

Not only streets, but boroughs and neighborhoods all through the city also keep the Dutch legacy. The Bronx is named after Jonas Bronck, a Swedish sea captain from the Netherlands, who bought the land in 1636 and built a farm there. Brooklyn and Harlem were named after cities in the Netherlands. The Bushwick area in Brooklyn was originally named *Boswijck* meaning "woods district," and Coney Island, *Conyne Eylandt*, also in Brooklyn, means "Rabbit Island."

Food items eaten in Stuyvesant's time are still popular today. Pretzels are loved so much that they are sold on most street corners. Beer and tavern life is also important to the fabric of the city, and New Yorkers still enjoy a good time.

After Stuyvesant lost the colony to the English, his fondness for the city caused him to stay. Stuyvesant's tense relationship with the colonists never prevented him from feeling at home in his colony. He retired to his farm and enjoyed life without official responsibility, gardening, and reading the Bible. He enjoyed watching

the family grow, and today the name of Stuyvesant has become part of the city. New York City named a school, an apartment complex, a park, and a statue in honor of this proud leader.

The most long lasting of Stuyvesant memories in New York is Stuyvesant himself. When he died in February 1672 on his *bouwery* (farm), at about the age of sixty-two, his body was carried the few steps from his house to the chapel and placed in a vault. This spot is now the site of St. Mark's Church, at Tenth Street and Second Avenue, and on the grounds is a sculptured bust of Stuyvesant. Stuyvesant Street, outside the chapel, is the only street on Manhattan Island that, if you were to look at a compass, actually runs in a due east-to-west direction. And it is said that if you are walking along this street on a very quiet night, you may hear the sounds of his silver leg.

Opposite: This bust of Peter Stuyvesant is located at St. Mark's Church in New York City where Stuyvesant's body was buried in 1672.

Timeline

1588   Defeat of the Spanish Armada by a combined force of English and Dutch.

1592?, 1602?, 1610? Peter Stuyvesant is born in Weststellingwerf, the Netherlands.

1602   Formation of the Dutch East India Company.

1609   Hudson, hired by the Dutch, sets sail in search of a northwest passage to Asia and reaches the river that now bears his name.

1614   The Dutch fur trader Hendrick Christiansen builds Fort Orange, near present-day Albany.

1620   Pilgrims land at Plymouth Rock, Massachusetts.

1621   The Dutch West India Company is formed.

1624   The Dutch West India Company sends the first settlers to New Netherland. New Amsterdam is founded as the capital of New Netherland.

1625   Willem Verhulst, the first director-general of New Netherland, arrives in New Amsterdam.

1626 Peter Minuit arrives in New Netherland as director-general to replace Verhulst.

1630 Peter Stuyvesant begins his studies at the University of Franeker.

1638 William Kieft becomes director-general of New Netherland.

1643 The Dutch West India Company promotes Peter Stuyvesant to director-general of the Dutch islands of Curaçao, Aruba, and Bonaire in the Caribbean.

1644 Peter Stuyvesant loses his right leg during a battle on the Caribbean island of St. Martin.

1645 Peter Stuyvesant marries Judith Bayard.

1647 Peter Stuyvesant arrives in New Netherland as director-general.

Stuyvesant's son Balthazar Lazarus is born.

1648 Stuyvesant's second son, Nicholas William, is born.

1650 Peter Stuyvesant negotiates the Treaty of Hartford with New England officials.

1651 English Parliament passes the Navigation Act, resulting in war between England and the Netherlands, usually called the First Anglo-Dutch War.

1654 England and the Netherlands agree to a truce,
called the Treaty of Westminster.

Fort Casimir on the Delaware River is captured
by Johan Rising, governor of New Sweden and
renamed Fort Trefaldighet (Fort Trinity).

Twenty-four Sephardic Jews arrive in New
Amsterdam, the first in North America.

1655 Stuyvesant reclaims Fort Trinity (Fort Casimir).

The Peach War breaks out between Indians and New
Amsterdam.

1657 Quakers of New Netherland draft the Flushing
Remonstrance demanding basic, individual rights. It is
recognized as the first declaration of religious tolerance
by any group of ordinary citizens in American history.

1664 The English take over New Amsterdam and rename it
New York.

Second Anglo-Dutch War erupts.

1667 Treaty of Breda is signed ending the Second
Anglo-Dutch War.

1672 Peter Stuyvesant dies in New Amsterdam.

Glossary

archives (AR-kyvs) A place where records or historical documents are kept.

bouwery, or bowery (BOWR-ee) A Dutch colonial plantation or farm.

colony (KAH-luh-nee) A large group of people who have left their own country to live in a new land but are still ruled by the leaders and laws of their old country.

curfew (KUR-fyoo) A set hour when certain people are required to be off the streets or at home.

deed (DEED) A signed document usually containing some legal transfer, bargain, or contract.

deplorable (dih-PLOR-uh-bul) Regrettable, or deserving of contempt.

dictatorial (dik-tuh-TOR-ee-uhl) Exercising complete control over others.

diligent (DIH-luh-junt) Characterized by steady, earnest, and energetic effort.

domineering (dom-ih-NEER-ing) Inclined to exercise overbearing control.

exploitation (ek-sploy-TAY-shun) An act or instance of making productive use of something to one's own advantage.

Golden Age (GOL-dun AYJ) A period of great happiness, prosperity, and achievement.

guilder (GIL-der) Dutch money or currency.

harbor (HAR-bur) A part of a body of water that is protected and deep enough to allow boats to anchor.

indigo (IN-dih-go) A blue dye from the indigo plant that was used to color cloth and other items.

indispensable (in-dih-SPEN-suh-buhl) Something that is absolutely necessary.

legacy (LEH-guh-see) Something that is passed down from one's ancestors.

mosaic (moh-ZAY-ik) A picture or scene made of many different and colorful pieces, or something resembling this.

Navigation Act (na-vuh-GAY-shun AKT) The name given to the British Acts of Trade. The acts were designed to expand the English ship trade, provide England with raw materials, and develop colonial markets for English manufacturers. The threat to English shipping posed by the Dutch led to the Navigation Act of 1651.

ordinance (OR-duh-nunts) A law set forth by a person in authority.

outpost (AUT-post) An outlying branch of a main organization or group used to protect land and conduct business.

persecution (pur-sih-KYOO-shun) The act of trying to injure a group because they are different especially in origin, religion, or social outlook.

petition (puh-TIH-shun) A formal written request made to a person of authority.

satirical (suh-TIR-ih-kul) Relating to a literary work that makes fun of people and society.

Sephardic (suh-FAR-dik) The branch of Jews that settled in Spain and Portugal and later in the Balkans, Brazil, the Netherlands, and America.

stockade (sto-KADE) A line of stout posts set firmly to form a defense, operating like a large fence.

Treaty of Hartford (TREE-tee UV HART-furd) An agreement signed in 1650 by the Dutch and the British colonies that determined the boundaries between New Netherland and New England.

Treaty of Westminster (TREE-tee UV WEST-minster) An agreement signed in 1654 by England

and the Netherlands calling a truce on the war over the Navigation Acts.

truce (TROOS) A suspension of fighting by agreement of the forces involved in the dispute.

wampum (WOM-pum) Beads made by the Indians of the Northeast from polished shells, often strung in strings, belts, or sashes and used as decoration, in trade, for gift giving, or for ceremonial occasions.

Additional Resources

To learn more about Peter Stuyvesant and the history of New York, check out these books and Web sites.

Books

Banks, Joan. *Peter Stuyvesant: Dutch Military Leader (Colonial Leaders)*. Edited by Arthur M. Schlesinger. New York: Chelsea House Publishers, 2000.

Costabel, Eva Deutsch. *The Jews of New Amsterdam*. New York: Simon & Schuster Children's, 1988.

Grumet, Robert S. *The Lenape*. Edited by Frank W. Porter. New York: Chelsea House Publishers, 1991

Hakim, Joy. *The History of U.S.: The First Americans, Vol. 1* New York: Oxford University Press, 1999

Web Sites

http://www.pbs.org/wnet/newyork/laic/episode1/e1_mm.html

http://www.newnetherland.org/

http://www.coins.nd.edu/ColCoin/ColCoinIntros/Netherlands.html

Bibliography

Brindell, Dennis Fradin. *The New York Colony.* New York: Children's Press, 1988.

Grumet, Robert S. *The Lenapes.* From the series *Indians of North America*, Frank W. Porter III, General Editor. New York: Chelsea House Publishers, 1989.

Kessler, Henry H. and Eugene Rachlis. *Peter Stuyvesant and His New York.* New York: Random House, 1959.

A Journey into Mohawk and Oneida Country, 1634–1635: The Journal of Harmen Meyndertsz van den Bogaert. Translated and edited by Charles T. Gehring and William A. Starna. New York: Syracuse University Press, 1988.

New Netherland Documents. Volume XVII. Edited by Charles T. Gehring and Dr. J. A. Schiltkamp. New York: Heart of the Lakes Publishing, 1987.

Index

About the Authors

L. J. Krizner is Director of Education at The New-York Historical Society in New York City. She develops programs in outreach education and integrates museum and classroom curriculum in a variety of American history topics. She has produced several curriculum guides for teachers on the use of primary resources in the classroom and has expanded curriculum on New York's seventeenth century history. She has co-curated two exhibitions, *Kid City* and *$24: The Legendary Deal for Manhattan*. L. J. earned her Master's degree in Museum Education from Bank Street Teachers College in New York City. This is her first book.

Lisa Sita is Educational Programs Coordinator for The Luce Center for the Study of American Culture at The New-York Historical Society, where she teaches and develops programs about American history and society. She was co-curator of the New-York Historical Society exhibition *$24: The Legendary Deal for Manhattan* and has written several books for children on American Indian culture and other topics. Lisa holds undergraduate and Master's degrees in anthropology.

Credits

Photo Credits

Pp. 4, 7, 8, 11, 18, 21, 22, 29, 32, 33, 36, 38, 50, 54, 55, 59, 62, 74 ©
Collection of the New-York Historical Society; p. 6 © Art Resource,
NY; pp. 12, 15, 17, 20, 24, 51, 61, 64, 69, 76, 79, 83, 84, 86, 89, 91 ©
North Wind Pictures; pp. 14 © Stock Montage/SuperStock; pp. 19,
23, 26 & 56 © Archive Photos; pp. 26, 90 & 92 © Archive
Photos/Hulton Getty; pp. 27, 28, & 41 (bottom) © Rochester
Museum and Science Center; p. 31 New York State Library; p. 35,
52, 67 © Bettman/CORBIS; pp. 41 (top): cat. no. 20.1/6541, 43: cat.
no. 20.0/1795 © American Museum of Natural History; pp. 46,
48–49, 57, 58, 66, 93, 94 © SuperStock; p. 80 © Musee Historique,
Versailles Palace/Explorer, Paris/SuperStock; p. 96 © Dallas and
John Heaton/CORBIS; p. 98 by Michelle Edwards.

Series Design and Layout

Laura Murawski

Project Editor

Joanne Randolph